Following
a Lark

GEORGE MACKAY BROWN

Following a Lark

Poems

JOHN MURRAY
Albemarle Street, London

© George Mackay Brown 1996

First published in 1996
by John Murray (Publishers) Ltd,
50 Albemarle Street, London W1X 4BD

The moral right of the author has been asserted

A catalogue record for this book is available from the British Library

ISBN 0–7195–5620–1

Typeset by Wearset, Boldon, Tyne and Wear

Printed and bound in Great Britain by The University Press, Cambridge

To
Magnus Dixon

Contents

Introduction

More than people who live in cities, perhaps, islanders
in the north and west are vividly aware of the sun and
its four stations through the year – the equinoxes and
the solstices. Many of the poems in this book are
celebrations of the sun, from its low brief midwinter arc
to its great fire celebrations at Johnsmas, at the zenith.
Springtime and Easter scatter the hills with lambs and
wild flowers and the cleansing 'muirburn'; in autumn
are the harvest homes, beside indoor fires, to celebrate
the inbringing of the corn: the innumerable children of
the sun. Every season has its fires, as if the children of
the sun were entreating the light to return from
darkness, to stay with them, to provide them with corn
and milk and fleeces through the lessening days of
autumn and winter. But in winter the stars go through
the night in huge rejoicing legions, and the changing
wick of the moon sheds enchantment wherever it looks.

Burns is the great poet of winter: but his winter
treasury spills out over the entire twelvemonth. I feel the
urge to write him a poem every January.

These poems are written mainly in praise of the light,
and to glorify in a small way the Light behind the light,
that gives life and meaning to all the creatures of earth.

George Mackay Brown
December 1995

church and norse
earl's palace

papa
westray

north
ronaldsay

sanday

pierowall

westray

calf
of
eday

kettletoft

eynhallow

rousay

egilsay

eday

papa
stronsay

brough
of birsay

birsay

Loch
of swannay

wyre

stronsay

twatt

Loch of Boardhouse

vestrafiold

mainland
(hrossey, isle of horses)

gairsay

Bay of skaill

scara brae

skelbrae

Dounby

sandwick

Loch of harray

yesnaby

Finstown

shapinsay

auskerry

ring of brodgar

maes howe

kirkwall

Loch of stenness

stones
of stenness

st ola

Cairston

deerness

innertown

stromness (hamnavoe)

orphir

st
andrews

copinsay

hoy sound

houton head

holm

kame of hoy

st john's
head

scapa
flow

lambholm
italian chapel

ward hill

graemsay

old man
of hoy

rackwick

fara

BURRAY

the kist

hoy

flotta

st margaret's hope

south
ronaldsay

Longhope

pentland firth

stroma

john o'groats

* churchill barriers

miles

| 0 | 5 | 10 | 15 | 20 |

| 0 | 8 | 16 | 24 | 32 |

kilometres

thurso

caithness

orkney

Following a Lark
A Country Boy Goes to School

1
There he is, first lark this year
    Loud, between
That raincloud and the sun, lost
Up there, a long sky run, what peltings of song!
    (Six times 6, 36. Six times 7, 42
    Six times eight is . . .)
Oh, Mr Ferguson, have mercy at arithmetic time
    On peedie Tom o' the Glebe.

2
There's Gyre's ewe has 2 lambs.
    Snow on the ridge still.
How many more days do I have to take
This peat under my oxter
    For the school fire?
(James the Sixth, Charles the First . . . Who then?)
Oh, Mr Ferguson, I swear
    I knew all the Stewarts last night.

3
Yes, Mistress Wylie, we're all fine.
    A pandrop! Oh, thank you.
I must hurry, Mistress Wylie,
    Old Ferguson
Gets right mad if a boy's late.
I was late twice last week.
    Do you know this, Mistress Wylie,
The capital of Finland is Helsingfors . . .
    Yes, I'll tell Grannie
You have four fat geese this summer.

4
When I get to the top of the brae
I'll see the kirk, the school, the shop,
        Smithy and inn and boatyard.
I wish I was that tinker boy
Going on over the hill, the wind in his rags.

Look, the schoolyard's like a throng of bees.

5
I wish Willie Thomson
        Would take me on his creel-boat!
'Tom, there's been six generations of Corstons
        Working the Glebe,
And I doubt there'll never be fish-scales
On your hands, or salt in your boots . . .'

(Sixteen ounces, one pound. Fourteen pounds, one stone.)
A sack of corn's a hundredweight.
        I think a whale must be bigger than a ton.

6
Jimmo Spence, he told me
        Where the lark's nest is.
        Beside a stone in his father's oatfield,
        The high granite corner.

('I wandered lonely as a cloud . . .' Oh where? What then?)

I could go up by the sheep track
        Now the scholars are in their pen
And *Scallop* and *Mayflower* are taking the flood
        And the woman of Fea
Is pinning her washing to the wind.

I could wait for the flutter of the lark coming down.

7
The school bell! Oh, my heart's
Pounding louder than any bell.

A quarter of a mile to run.
My bare feet
Have broken three daffodils in the field.

Heart thunderings, last tremor of the bell
And the lark wing-folded.

'Late again, Master Thomas Corston of Glebe farm.
Enter, sir. With the greatest interest
We all await your explanation
Of a third morning's dereliction.'

A Boy in a Snow Shower

Said the first snowflake
No, I'm not a shilling,
I go quicker than a white butterfly in summer.

Said the second snowflake
Be patient, boy.
Seize me, I'm a drop of water on the end of your finger.

The third snowflake said,
A star?
No, I've drifted down out of that big blue-black cloud.

And the fourth snowflake,
Ah good, the road
Is hard as flint, it tolls like iron under your boots.

And the fifth snowflake,
Go inside, boy,
Fetch your scarf, a bonnet, the sledge.

The sixth snowflake sang,
I'm a city of sixes,
Crystal hexagons, a hushed sextet.

And the trillionth snowflake,
All ends with me –
I and my brother Fire, we end all.

Maeshowe: Midwinter

Equinox to Hallowmas, darkness
    falls like the leaves. The
    tree of the sun is stark.

On the loom of winter, shadows
    gather in a web; then the
    shuttle of St Lucy makes a
    pause; a dark weave
    fills the loom.

The blackness is solid as a
    stone that locks a tomb.
    No star shines there.

Then begins the true ceremony of
    the sun, when the one
    last fleeting solstice flame
    is caught up by a
    midnight candle.

Children sing under a street
    lamp, their voices like
    leaves of light.

Gray's Pier

I lay on Gray's pier, a boy
And I caught a score of sillocks one morning

I laboured there, all one summer
And we built the *Swan*

A June day I brought to my door
Jessie-Ann, she in white

I sang the Barleycorn ballad
Between a Hogmanay star and New Year snow

The *Swan* haddock-heavy from the west –
Women, cats, gulls!

I saw from the sea window
The March fires on Orphir

I followed, me in black
Jessie-Ann to the kirkyard

I smoke my pipe on Gray's pier now
And listen to the Atlantic

sillocks: young coalfish

One Summer in Gairsay Isle

1 Ivor

The wings, leaning south, this April morning,
The beat of a sail, the lessening cry of the helmsman.
I that left my good arm in Ireland,
That assault on the keep,
Now I am going up from the shore
To study, all summer, corn-growth
And have my two ears washed
With women's words, all summer
(Ragna kneels, silent, at a rockpool)
And see all summer
Old men and boys rowing to creels.
All summer I must keep cows from the oatfield.
I can still fling a falcon on the gale.

Those who come back for harvest,
The ghosts who do not come back
At Lindisfarne fallen, or under a cliff in Brittany,
I am at ease with them.
I can drink with the living
And hear praise of the lost sailors, in winter.
I will not be despised
When the ship is furled in the shed like a golden bird
And the women fold themselves
In a decent silence, among looms and cheese moulds.

All but I will go out then with sickles.
Ragna will follow, bending and binding.

2   *The Girl*

That young broken Ivor,
I will go to his hut.
In the morning I'll lay and light his fire.

The hurt in his eye
On the hill, at the peat-bank,
Along the boat-cluttered shore!

The women of Gairsay
Bake, brew, weave for him.
They leave (unthanked) the offerings at his door.

I am not too ugly a girl,
I long to put honey in his mouth,
I would draw a comb through the blown corn of his
hair.

Hild and Thora, those girls
Scatter the sweet looks all about him.
He curls his lip like a cur.

He will say the good word to one creature only,
His hawk hung
In torrents of high blue air.

3   *The Old Woman in the Kirk*

Here I am again with my few candles
Lady.
Let the corn have gentle falls
Of sun and wind and rain.
Let my old Thord bring in a few lobsters from under
Scabra.

Ploughmen and shepherds
Are in the south again, in Sweyn's longship.
Let them not
Be washing their hands in too much gold and fire.

I pray, let the winter
Lie not too heavy on me and old Thord.
There is nothing so fine
As your face, Lady, above the seven small flames.

Saint Magnus will bid you often
Be good to his folk in the cold islands.
I am lighting a candle now
For one-armed Ivor and for Ragna
Married today by the Eynhallow monk.

The Journey

The spirit summons out of chaos
Galaxies
And sun moon stars
Then a tree with an apple and a bird,
A river with a fish,
A place of grass for lions and gazelles.

At last a man, a woman, a son and a daughter

All danced together,
The planets, mountains, forests, waters, islands, beasts,
folk.

God said,
'All things I leave in your hands, man,
For praise and profit
But never leave the dance.'

In the end the man turned from the music.
He studied numbers.
He forged a key to open the golden door of the sun.

Let a path be made now by his children
From his ruined house, under
The apple tree, under
The broken scroll of the stars.
Let him set out, with the girl before him, guiding him.
(He is blind from the sun-probing)
His hand a withered leaf.

'On the far side of the hill
A boy will come with a lantern.
He will take us to the inn, father' . . .
A table was set with bread and bottle and lamp.
He danced there, old man, on sun-scarred feet.

Crossing the Alps

Macbeth King of Scotland and
Thorfinn Sigurdson Earl of Orkney

What should I say to Pope Clement?
   I do not know what I shall say
     Till the confession screen
Is there between us. Will it matter

If the Bishop of Rome doesn't understand
   My Gaelic, nor I his Latin?
     In truth, cousin, I hardly
Understand your Danish, but for

The courtesy and kindness that
   Flashes between us now and then
     Brighter than the high snows
We have ridden through since morning.

What should I say? I have killed a king.
   But in every court, from
     Scotland to India, powerful men
Stalk still like wolves in the forest

And Macbeth is marked in his turn
   For knife or poisoned cup.
     Besides, that king was weak
And the ordering of such beasts

Calls for puissance in sceptre and crown.
   The hands of the princes
     Frail as garden flowers.
Moreover, a nation needs a queen,

A strong mother to succour innocence.
   Sir, when I left Inverness, Gruath
     Walked many nights with a candle.
We will light heavenly candles for her

In the hundred churches of Rome.
I have moreover this sack of pence
To throw to the wayside poor.
Cousin, we have come to such friendship

On those perilous snow passes
I know you will prevail on those
Norwegian wolf-ships,
The men from the bays, Vikings, away

From our settled Scottish coasts, now
I am threatened from south
By the Saxons, from west
By the savages from Lewis and Argyll,

And your tables will never lack
Salmon and Speyside usque
Nor Ingibiorg your countess
Go without our cairngorms and silver.

Was there not Babel, the thousand
Tongues? There's an angel
Carries a heart's true sorrow
From penitent tongue to priestly ear

Urgent as the pleading of David's harp
And the answer falls
Purer than dew, silent
As manna in the desert. Look, cousin,

A gap of blue between the mountains.
The groom goads the mule no more.
Shall we halt beside this torrent?
The road winds down to orchards and vineyards.

To a Hamnavoe Poet of 2093

Language unstable as sand, but poets
    Strike on hard rock, carving
    Rune and hieroglyph, to celebrate
      Breath's sweet brevity.

Swan-path, whale-acre. Do you honour
    The sea with good images?
    We wear the sea like a coat,
      We have salt for marrow.

I hoard, before time's waste
    Old country images: plough-horse,
    Skylark, grass-growth,
      Corn-surge, dewfall, anvil;

Rain-trail from hill to hill, a hushing;
    Mayburn a penny whistle
    Lilting from Croval, lingering
      (Tinker-boy) under my window;

Creel-scattering gales; Thor's
    Hammer, studdering, on Hoy.
    Do your folk laugh and cry
      With the gentle ups-and-downs

Not so different, I think
    From talk in Skarabrae doors,
    Celtic shepherds at Gurness,
      Sweyn's boatmen off Gairsay?

The masque unchanging, the maskers
    Wear different motley.
    'Ox' is 'tractor' now
      On the green surge of Fea.

So, image maimed more and more
On the grid of numbers
Folk must not forget
The marks on the rock.

Keep vigil. The tongues flow yet
To rhythms of sea and hill.
Deeper than stone, guard
The pure source, silence.

studdering: reverberating

Anne Bevan, Sculptor
Hills, Woolcraft, Stone

'Good' said God as he made the
    wind, the sea, the fire, the
    folded hills

'Good' said the shepherd as he
    fleeced his flock

'Good' said the wife at the hearthstone
    spinning wool on her wheel

'Good' said the weaver as the shuttle
    clacked

'Good' said the housewife as she
    folded blankets in a basket, fresh
    from sun and wind

'Good' said the quarryman as he
    hewed a great stone from
    the mountain

'Good' said the sculptor as she
    made her sculpture

*

To make things is to do well

*

And to do things in harmony, all
    trades and images cohering, is
    to catch time and form in their
    flight, until all cry *Gloria*

15

A New Child: ECL
11 June 1993

i

Wait a while, small voyager
    On the shore, with seapinks and shells.

The boat
    Will take a few summers to build
That you must make your voyage in.

ii

You will learn the names.
That golden light is 'sun' – 'moon'
    The silver light
That grows and dwindles.

And the beautiful small splinters
    That wet the stones, 'rain'.

iii

There is a voyage to make,
    A chart to read,
But not yet, not yet.
        'Daisies' spill from your fingers.
        The night daisies are 'stars'.

iv

The keel is laid, the strakes
    Will be set, in time.
A tree is growing
    That will be a tall mast.

All about you, meantime
The music of humanity,

16

The dance of creation
Scored on the chart of the voyage.

v

The stories, legends, poems
Will be woven to make your sail.

You may hear the beautiful tale of Magnus
    Who took salt on his lip.
Your good angel
    Will be with you on that shore.

vi

Soon, the voyage of EMMA
    To Tir Nan Og and beyond.

vii

Star of the Sea, shine on her voyage.

A Rainy Johnsmas
23 June: The Hill Fire

Jeremiah, Fisherman

Heavy showers for a week,
Wind nor-east
In the light lengthening.

Not a star.

I think it's the old dinghy, *Simon*, for axe and fire.
She's been a hen-house now, twenty years.

Maisie of Quoys

What does an old done wife
    Want with a cradle?

Two grown sons, five married daughters
    In Selskay, Canada, Hamnavoe.
Grandbairns along hill and shore
    Come and go like birds.

Take axe to crib, Maisie
    For the longest-day fire.

The bonny burn songs
    Lost, this June, with cloud slurpings.

Minister

The new minister says
    'No paganism from now on.
Johnsmas, that's papish.

I'm sure the Baptist never saw fire
Other than the desert sun
And maybe the small invisible flame
    He roasted locusts on . . .'

But Rev Murdo Keith
    Made no move to stop us
When we went with sacks of red peat,
    A bucket of tar, past the Manse.

Cover the kindling with a patched sail –
    Three days of rain now.

Maggie, Spinster

Fire! I want to see no more fires for ever
After the ale-fire and bread-fire
    I slaved over,
Beer a month, bannocks a week,

To keep the dance in the dancers
On the top of Fea,
The boys leaping like goats,
Flames washing the soles of their flying feet.

Four drenched bairns at the door
'Maggie, have you a few sticks, if you please, for the
                                             fire?'

School-master

Gifts of the crowned sun,
    Horses, bee-hives, bread
(We think fish
    Circle and surge with the moon
And fish-oil fills the winter lamps.)

No lamp in the crofts on Johnsmas Eve.

The scarecrow in Maggie's field
    Has a dark dripping sleeve.

The Guardian

St John the Baptist, you stood in the Jordan.
Purest water fell from your hands.
Bless our fire tonight. Bless
    The demptions of rain.

Creator of sun, moon, stars
He stood with John among river rainbows.
    He later walked among hills
And dried his coat at fires
And read by a small lamp at midnight.

The Light of the World
    Broke bread with fisher folk.

The poor folk of an island
    Honour you, St John.
Tomorrow's the brightest day of the year.

What's a raindrop or two in the long grass?
    A lucent trembling orb.

Mansie's Wife

This Johnsmas Eve
    Fewer dancers than last year.
A hundred fewer on the hill-top
    Since Mansie, the oldest dancer
    (He threw down cap and stick

And hobbled, ale-flown,
        A sunward step or two)
Was dandled, a bairn,
In flame shadows and sunset.

The two fiddlers went home
        Drenched, early.

The young laird says, 'Another rain-storm
And their corn will be green mush!'

                    *

The Johnsmas Fire
Was never lit on Fea again.

demptions: heavy rain-showers

21

Black Thorbjorn

'In Acre, sickness broke out in the ship's company, and many men of note died, including Thorbjorn the Black, Iceland poet'
Orkneyinga Saga

1

The best poets live in Iceland.
I have a farm there.
It is a long house – cows
Winter in one end.
        At the other end, barn and kiln.
I have been known to scythe hayfields.
        I've put a ring in a bull's nose.
But men say, behind their hands
'Thorbjorn with the black beard
Is the worst farmer in Broadfirth'.

2

I said to my father,
        'The wife you are bringing here for me
        Let her be good with horses.
        She must have strong shoulders
To row the boat to the salmon.
I expect good goat cheeses,
        Ale that comes brisk from the keg
To marry with honey' . . .

I must give my strength
        To the welding of rune and kenning.

Lo, with the dowry (a hundred silver pieces)
Has come this mingy creature
        With wheel and coloured wools.

3
A ship from the Baltic,
    Two French priests, a Flemish deacon
    Wine, tapestries for the cathedral.

Their word is, Rognvald of Orkney
    Will be Jerusalem-faring, come spring.

Rognvald of Orkney, poet, earl, skipper
    Wants poets for five ships.
He'll get cut-throats, roof-burners,
    Icon-breakers, drouths
(But generally those Orkney seamen
Can set a sail to drink wind
    From the edges of a storm.)

4
It is a fortunate thing, I have here
    At the farm Oykell
    A good cattle-man, a passable shepherd,
Two butter and cheese girls

And a rheumaticky uncle
That still has a way with crab-creels,

    Or Thorbjorn the poet
Would be a beggar in his own farm

Distracted from the difficult craft of verse
    By this butterfly of a bride.

drouths: drunkards

23

5
I took two dowry mintings. I passed
    A week in a Reykjavik tavern
    Mostly drunk, with Ubi, Oddi, Arni,
    Poets from the fjords.

We sang, boasted, quarrelled.
    Ubi's harp a tangle of oak and wires at midnight.

'Good skalds are voyagers,
    Drinkers of gale and battle' . . .

'No, but the storm of images
Draws the mind beyond Rus or Markland
    Though the poet
Never leaves circle of lamplight' . . .

Then this sleaze of a taverner,
    'Thorbjorn, sir, the two silver pence
    Were exhausted
With the last clash of your ale-cups,

And Oddi, glacier poet
Has broken a valuable carved horn'.

6
I said to my butterfly
    'Let your brothers come! Let
The graybeard come, the father, a rascal
Tore fields from twelve poor men
    To build a long hall at Eshaness.
In Thorbjorn's farm
    A wife must be early at cheeseboard,
    Beehive, spinning wheel, hearthstone,
Not dimpling daylong upon needles and coloured wools,
Not destroying the silence
    Skald or monk must wear about him always'.

24

7
Ragnhild, butterfly, out and off
    Across glacier, across
The burning mountain. But back
    Before the first snow. 'Thorbjorn,
I intend to be now a thrifty wife.
I can make a pot of ox-broth.
Look, Thorbjorn, the reddened arms
    From baking, steeping clothes!'

By then, my sea-chest was roped.
Ubi, Oddi, Arni
    Stood shuffling at the byre wall,
Harps on shoulders.
    Bishop with crozier on the shore stones.
Sail fluttered at *Raven*'s mast.

The milk girls wept in the byre door.

'My Ragnhild, you have done well.
    I will bring you
    A bolt of red silk from Paris.
I will pray for my farm-wife
    In the kirks of Byzantium.
Ragnhild, honey-bee, expect your wordman
In five years, or six, or whenever'.

Winter and Summer

1
The old scant-silver King,
Ice axes
Have hewn him down.

Give him to the ocean.
Lay in the ship his long bones.

The death ship burns, south-west horizon, early
afternoon.

2
The world's winter.
Twelve old folk
Have followed their king
But into an earth-wave, a howe.

But you, old crofter-fisherman
Sit at your smouldering peats awhile.
Ponder time. Be patient.

3
So the Norse skalds: an end
In ice and fire, Earth

A bitter drop in an ocean of numbers,
Lost note in a music beyond understanding.

howe: burial mound

4
Ploughmen break furrows
　　　　But for more graves.

There are no fires
　　　　When fishermen's throats
　　　　Are blocked with salt, westward.

5
Fountains of light, never. Flamings
　　　　Of the last fire, drifted
　　　　Flakes of snowdrop, crocus, rose.

6
The drowned King,
Left the stone wreck at midnight. He stood
　　　　Knee-deep in daffodils.

Soon tongues of fire
　　　　Made poets of all the fishers and ploughmen.

7
Midsummer. The ascended King
　　　　Stores the island
With honey and green corn.

Fiddles, a dance on the hill,
　　　　A midnight fire.

And the ship veers
　　　　Towards the islands shaped like loaves.

A Calendar of Kings

They endured a season
Of ice and silver swans.

Delicately the horses
Grazed among snowdrops.

They traded for fish, wind
Fell upon crested waters.

Along their track
Daffodils lit a thousand tapers.

They slept among dews.
A dawn lark broke their dream.

For them, at solstice
The chalice of the sun spilled over.

Their star was lost.
They rode between burnished hills.

A fiddle at a fair
Compelled the feet of harvesters.

A glim on their darkling road.
The star! It was their star.

In a sea village
Children brought apples to the horses.

They lit fires
By the carved stones of the dead.

A midwinter inn.
Here they unload the treasures.

Winter: An Island Boy

A snowflake
Came like a white butterfly on his nose.

His mother's bucket
Was blue splashings at the well.

And grandpa
Was notching hooks like stars on his lines
Down at the noust.

The school locked for Yule
– Time was a bird with white wings.

A swan on the loch
Bent its head like a flower.

He was lost on the hill till sundown
In a dream of snow.

Hunger and lamplight
Led the wanderer home.

A black peat, stirred
Unsheathed claws like a cat
On the purring hearth.

One white star
Walked slow across the pane.

noust: boat shelter

St Peter and St Paul

1
Here where I write poems,
Three generations ago
A clerk
Wrote invoices in a ledger, concerning
 Consignments of 'Old Orkney' whisky.
He headed each letter
Stromness Distillery, June the 29th, 1900

2
The boats were in from the west.
 The seven fishermen
Had sold their haddocks along the street,
 Threepence a pound,
Weighing the fish on brass hand-scales.
The calendar
Behind Billy Clouston's bar counter
 Is ringed June 29.
Flett's ale is twopence the schooner
 To the scaled and salted fishermen.

3
An old blind man
Sits on a bench on a pier in the sun.
 He has thumbed his bible
Cover to cover, more than once
And he knows Peter
 Better than the famous whalers of his youth,
And Paul blinded with glory
On a road a bit like the road to Kirkwall
 (Not the drifting webs
 That dimmed his sea-wrinkled eyes)

But this summer day he doesn't see
    Today is the Feast of Peter and Paul.

4
Mrs Ross, postmistress
    Date-stamps her little flock of letters
'Stromness, 29 June 1900'.
    A postman – my father maybe –
Will take them in a sealed bag
    Down to the mail-boat 'St Ola'.

And the birds will fly
    To Birsay, Edinburgh, St Johns, Sydney.

And Mrs Ross ponders letters with exotic stamps:
    'San Pedro', 'Sao Paulo'.

5
'This on the haddock's gills'
    Says Sinclair, fisherman, to a tourist
Sketching his boat and pier
Is Peter's fingerprints'.

But Peter's fingerprint on the living silver
Is too small for the water-colour.

    And Paul is a sea-echo only
To a far-travelled wealthy amateur artist.

6
Captain Halcro, skipper,
    Takes snuff, tells the minister
    Yes, indeed, he knows the waters
    St Paul sailed over, the rock
Paul shipwrecked on, in Malta.

31

Captain James Halcro
Has a very fine house behind the ramshackle town.
He dines frequently
With Mr Rae at Clestrain and Mr Thom, Sheriff.

At each month's end
He visits Peter Halcro, fisherman,
    At the door they were born in, twins
Sixty-two years ago.

A pound. 'For twine, not rum, man . . .'

7
The kirk an old fisherman
    Will be buried from today
Is called St Peter's.

The globe-girdling ocean,
St Paul's waves peal forever
    On the beach below the kirkyard.

And tomorrow is the Feast of Peter and Paul.

The Old Wife and the Hill Folk

What were they that passed my door?
      A shower
     Hid them from me.
     A few shapes only in the cloud I could see

At the end of the road, as they went
      Slow and bent
     On up the hill
     Past the fold, into the last of the outspill

And whisper of rain. They were
      The tinker
     And his bairns and pony
     Loaded with kettles, going on to their stony

Hollow from the Hamnavoe Fair.
      Oh, I fear
     The fated folk
     Who'll stand round my bed soon with cinders
      and a glimmering wick.

Lux Perpetua

A star for a cradle

Sun for plough and net

A fire for old stories

A candle for the dead

*

Lux perpetua
By such glimmers we seek you.

Five Christmas Stars

1 *Spinning Wheel*

The wheel utters a long gray line.
    An old woman
    Is turning her wheel at the fire.

The sun goes behind the hill.
    She lights her lamp.
    The wool lies in a drift on the floor.

Some winter morning
    She'll waken to a web of whitest wool
    Hung over the tall straw chair

For a bridal or a christening
    Or for a shrouding at harvest.

2 *Bairn Song*

What does Dapple say in the byre?

Dapple says
    'They give me turnips and hay by lantern-light.
    Last summer
    God gave me grass and clover,
    Sun, wind, a blue sky, a green hill, dew in the
                              morning
    And I gave them milk butter cheese.'

That's what Dapple's saying,
Bairn
In the byre on Yule morning.

3 Stars and Fish

The sky shoal is out tonight,
    Stars in a surge!

Two fish on a blue plate
Suffice
For one croft, for the great world-hunger.

4 Solstice

'How shall we know
The sun
Won't grow weaker and frailer yet
Till he's the dead King
With hair frail as snowflakes
And a star locked in his eye?' . . .

In the croft ben-room
A bairn sleeps
Through a night of storm and star-gifts.

5 Star

No more fishing till after Yule.
Haddock
    Will glimmer silent through cold gray halls.
The tractor is locked in the barn
With a sack of seed.

The hill humps like a white whale.

The glim of one star
    On a shore boulder, where the ebb begins.

Homage to Burns

1 *Hebridean*

'A book of poems is it?'
    Said the old man in Uist.
'When was it ever known
Songs between boards like caged birds?

Tell me more about this Burns –
    Has the wild rose
    Spilled over his hand ever, like heart's-blood?

The oppressor and the hypocrite,
Has he driven them, with bitter laughter, out of the
                                                    glen?

Has he run his eye along ploughshare
    And broacher of blood, those edges?

But poetry should be given on the wind, like a lark or a
                                                    falcon'.

2 *Minister*

Rev Wᵐ Clouston of Stromness:
One box books
From McCriven, booksellers, in the Canongate of
                                        Edinburgh.

The carter goes away with his fee.

Mr Clouston: 'Pope's *Iliad*,
Not a patch, I warrant, on the far-horizoned Greek,

But worthy the perusal.
Blair. Rousseau. Shenstone.
What, here? *Poems and Songs Mainly in the Scottish*
Dialect . . .

Yes, Jane, the snuff-horn.
And light, if you please, that lamp on the table.

3 Skipper

What, Simpson, what's that they're singing below?
What – repeat, please –
'A man's a man for a' that' . . .
There will be none of that Jacobinry on this ship.
Tell them, find better words.
A man
May be king or beggar, Simpson,
It's better so, every man
Locked in his place in the great music of society.
It was thus from the beginning of things.

A man's a man for a' that
On this ship a man is a sailor
And Simpson, I am the skipper.

4 Bride's Father

Lermontov. Byron. Burns.
The poets
Drop fruits from the great tree of poetry,
Lemon, pineapple, pear
And the roots locked in the hearts of men.

The Scotsmen,
Their poems are the wild sweet berries that purple the
                                                    tongue.

Adieu for evermore, my dear . . .

Even here, in Petersburg
As the coach comes to take Nadia away.

5   *Sugar Planter*

'To Rob! Burns, Mauchline, Ayrshire, Scotland –'

There's no such place as Scotland more,
Write, 'North Britain'.

Has written poems, has he?

Rest assured, Mr Burns will write no poems in Jamaica,
Mr Robert Burns
Will be too taken up with account books, ledgers.
Here the black slaves do the singing.

Proceed 'Dear Sir,
We are in receipt of your letter of application of 16th
                                                    ult' . . .

6   *Professor*

Was at the professor's last night, was he,
The rustic bard?
I thought Professor Blackie
Might open his door to worthier guests.

Here is one professor of law
Will not be entertaining
The wild warbler from the west.

Mr MacAndrew, listen.
The cloak of poetry is ancient and rich and jewel-
                                    encrusted.
It is not to be hung on a scarecrow between
The plough and the sickle.

7   *A Looker into the Seeds of Time*

In the starswarm is a world
In that world is a country
In that country is a mountain
In that mountain is a quarry
In that quarry is a stone
On that stone is a name

        The stone lacks chisel yet
        That quarry is unbroken yet
        The mountain has no root yet
        The country is the floor of a lake
        The world is a wheel of dust and fire,
        It turns
        Through chaos, blackness, silence.

        Now read the rune of the stone
        ROBERT BURNS POET

The Lords of Hell and the Word
A Poem for Burns Day

1
Stop every bard, poet, versifier,
    Tragedian, laureate, balladman.
Too many have slipped through
        To stand always in the choirs of Light.

Sift them, dust by ash.
    There should be no song in the urn.
The reports came in, in thousands.
        Only a whisper now and then,
            A sigh through the skull
Lost soon among root and rut.

2
Sir, a sailor lost,
        No dust songs, salt in his throat.
        His last Atlantic cry
A call to a girl on the far shore,
        A shout between two waves.

Is this a poem?

We may have lost that faceless one,
        He crossed over with such a vivid mouth.

3
Frail lamps of clay, the Light is in them.
        Jars of clay, they keep
A handful of the threshed winnowed grain.
Clay flutes, their flawed chambers echo
        The original Word.

41

So, for all their droopings to dust,
　　Our lordly Lie is never complete.

We have uttered winter on earth, centuries long.
　　A ploughman
Seeks, in his barn, with a lantern
　　A warped plough,
His flesh, graining to sure dust
Transfigured with hopeful harvest dances.

How, in such brutish clay
　　To set our subtle black sentence . . .

4
We have our eyes, lord
　　On a young farmer
With a liking for fiddles and girls
　　And verses in chapbooks.
　　He rhymes in a ledger in his father's attic.

We know his kind well.
Seedsmen's bills, worm in the corn,
　　Taxman in May and November
Tear the strings from the mouth, soon enough.

Leave the Ayrshire rustic
　　To the rusts and rots of a few winters.

5
Lord, a young man in Vienna
　　Slipped by us two days ago.
　　We saw pauper clods
Thudding down on the coffin.

Another boy has come
　　To another attic in Vienna.
A dark-browed leveller: Beethoven.

Block his hearing. Choke
    The pure runnels of song – strike
The music-man deaf!

6
Question every caller, every long silence
    At the kirkyard gate.
If the mouth
Has uttered bitterness at the end,
    Denial, hate, hunger
    For more goods, gear, gold
Near the tollgate of death
    The man is ours, poet or pauper or pilgrim
And the seamless Song poorer by a talter.

Sir, the bards are few on earth now.
Since that German engraver
    Cut Gothic letters on wood-blocks
Maggots
    Scrithe by millions in the corpse of Language.

7
Sir, the farmer you said, *Ignore him*
    He stood against his troubles,
Debt, poverty, defamation,
    Blaze of flattery, a last painful
    Stooping to dust,

And the harp of his mouth
    Stronger, winter by winter.

Against such radiance in the clay
    Our lanterns were black.

43

We have lost the farmer-poet, I think.

We will try diminishment now
    With couthy quotes, skirlings, haggis suppers.

scrithe: proliferate

February

I
How will he be remembered
    The old king, Winter?
In offices, barracks, libraries the whisper 'In this reign
    Evil walks through the land,
Children hollow, the face of age is stark, fishermen
Challenge the impossible west,
His tax-men trench
    The last corn sacks, a wolf
Slinks through the city square at moonrise.'

So the best minds conspired
By candle-light, behind locked doors.

'We know the tyrant has gone up now
    To his highest castle, beside eagles.'

II
To the eagle-watching king, in the high battlement
Have ridden six doctors
Besides the one trusted royal physician,
Breathers on the ruddiness in cinders,
    Bringers of the poppy,
One to still for an hour the shifting bone-rack.

Majesty shows itself, thrice in the day
Lest the fowlers and foresters
And the folk in the high snow village say
    'Is this true, that our king is sick?'
    'No. For we saw him on his horse this morning, up
                near the torrent'.

III
The old laureate wrote on his page –
'This king will be remembered for cruelty and coldness,
For stern performance, which is love.

Did the tax-man trouble the sack of seed corn?

The thrush throbbed on a snow bough
The root will raise a green fountain
Through the ruined tree of kings.

Logs are brought to winter fires,
Ice is broken at the well.

The king lies in the frosts and fires of time
That a poor peasant
Might bring betimes a sickle to cornstalks.'

IV
Rumour is, the enemy is in movement again, in the
                                                    south,
In the forest, among bird marshes.
It was said, a few tribes of bandits only.

A flag, trumpets, soldiers with skis and guns
        Would uproot the outlaws.
The column has not come home yet.
One, a deserter, was seized
Drinking wine that tasted of tar
In a sea tavern.
'They carried branches', said the man before he was
                                                    shot.
        'Their guns were wreathed in flowers,
        We fled from the sun on their foreheads.
        They unlocked the frozen waterfall . . .'

46

The veterans have received notice, the heroes
Of November and December.
So it is rumoured. It will take more than leaves
To overcome our guardsmen.

V
The old king has trouble in sleeping, now.
He has asked the chancellor's boy
        To read the Iceland stories,
Njal, Grettir, the Vinlanders,
        Men who hoarded light like silver
Between the two darknesses

The better to relish ale and wolf meat
        At the Feast of Solstice.
(One sits at the high seat, hooded, a stranger)
Silver rings are given to guest and stranger.

'Sire, here are urgent missives from the fortress . . .'

'Sire, the chaplain has come with missal and oil . . .'

VI
The seal of the master-shipwright, broken
        'Sire, the carpenters fitted the last strake yesterday,
        A bronze battering.
        The figurehead has its inlay of ore,
        Its golden look will burn the horizon haar.
        Sire, the Trondheim carvers
        Have rimmed the hull with tree runes.
        Women sat all winter
        At the weaving of the one broad sail.
        The mead jars are shipped now, sufficiency of
                                        loaves.
        Thwarts are of the best oak,
        The mast a single pine from the snow-line.

Lacketh not anything now
But loosened ropes, the dripping anchor
That majesty might stand with helmsman soon,
                    looking to westward,
To Hesper, away from this shore of exile'.

VII
The grand-daughter of the king
    Lights her lamp late in the afternoon now.
A month ago
The yellow circle was thrown early
On her page, on her sewing-frame.

In a little glass on the high sill
    The gardener has set fresh snowdrops.

She knows that her reign will not be long.

When the first star looks through her window
    Then she will seek out the old king
    Up and around and along the labyrinth.
    She will put her mouth
    To the quiet flung storm of his beard.

Daffodil Time

1 *Daffodils*

Ho, Mistress Daffodil, said Ikey (tinker)
Where have you been all winter?
There was snow in the ditches last night
And here you are.
Did you light your lamp in that blizzard?

When Ikey came back
Next day, with his pack, from windy Njalsay
The yellow hosts
Were cheering and dancing all the way to the inn.

2 *Idle Brute*

That idle brute of a man of hers
– Jean's phrase –
Has gone to the garden shed this morning
Instead of to the *Arctic Whaler*.
And Jock has scraped
Rust and cobwebs off a spade
And there he stands, idle ale-man, in the sun
Leaning on the spade, eyeing
That square of sodden sand and clay.

After his broth and fish
He asks Jean for half-a-crown.
'For drink? Nothing doing' . . .
'For seed tatties from the village shop, woman.'

3 Stone

The stone that wore darkness like the minister's coat
All winter,
Where the crow furled, where
Snow lingered longest –
    Look, now, sunrise
    Is tilting its jar of light over the world
    And now, this noon,
    A random splash has hit the winter stone.

4 School

In the island school
The children's heads
Are like green sheaths that will open soon.

And one of the seven shadows
Has left Mr McSween's face.

A lark glitters out song along the lift of the hill
And the bird
Is louder today than the chanted
Multiplication table.

And the globe of the world
In the dark corner, has a splash of light.

And Mr McSween says, like
A solemn song, 'This
Afternoon the Easter holiday begins
But now, again – and better this time – the three times
                             table' . . .

And twenty-one faces
Open like daffodils.

5 *Monastery*

Monkerhouse, is this it,
The ruin among the tombstones
Where once
The sanctuary light glowed like a ruby
And the sanctus bell
Beckoned, from winter, corn folk and fish folk?

Hoy Sound
Swallowed the good stones long ago.

Four and a half centuries
In the angels' hour-glass
Are but a whisper of time between
Good Friday and Easter morning.

The sea will give up its dead
The rock will break into cornstalks
The drowned bell will cry:
    Laudate dominum in sanctuario.

6 *The Ruin*

Scollie, Baltic merchant, he built the house,
Clean new stone,
A garden with roses and hives.

When does a house begin to rot?
After the blessing
Flies out like a bird, then
The strongest house is open to worm and rot.

Smiley, lawyer, lived here. Eunson,

Grocer and smuggler,
Stewart, a poor dominie
    (For three generations
    Not a child laughed in the long hall),
Smith the carter,
Ronaldson with trauchled wife and twelve bairns,
All kept by the poor fund.

That grand house,
It's like a skull for thirty years now.

Strangers – who? – have bought the ruin.
I saw, last Sabbath,
A new rooftree inside the walls.

7   *Spring Blizzard*

An April northerly. I sit
In the lee of the crag
Tarring my yole, *Charity*.

Another flake flurry – old Bessie Millie
Plucking her hens. I sit
In the lee of a rock
    Tarring this yole, *Charity*.

trauchled: bedraggled
yole: fishing-boat

Spring: The Kids of Feaquoy Farm

1
And one day after school
    The lamp stood gray on the dresser
        That had lit all teatimes since October.

Willie dug his horn spoon in his egg.
    Strange he thought it, the dead lamp
        But he said nothing.

A leaf of light
    Opened in the branches of his blood.

2
Saturday. Maggie astray on the hill.
    What's the faltering light
Beside Peg the old ewe?
    One knock-kneed lamb.
And they'd marked old Peg
    For one last fleece,
        For a few smoked scrag-ends and chops.

3
The island hill was scarved in smoke,
    The cleansing muirburn.
Tom found a first daisy beside a stone.
    Was the rooted granite
        Guarding the fragile earth-flame,
        Or had the daisy
A message from the dead to the stubborn rock?

    That night
The burning hill Fea washed out the stars.

4
A shroud of darkness from north.
'Lambing snow,' says an old farmer.

Anna could see
Neither Bu nor boats nor the next croft
    Through the dark surges.
Flakes clung to the window of Feaquoy,
    A thousand glimmering moths.

A blue sky chasm soon!
There, on the island loch,
    Twelve dingy swans.

The tractor up to the axle in a drift.

And father in from the byre
    With cheeks like turnip lanterns.

5
Miss Simpson, teacher
    Has a jar of daffodils on her desk.
Wilma brought the tight buds, drooping.
They open, flower by flower.
That stern stone face
    Is lit, between history and sums.

6
Old Merran's score of Rhode Islands
    Are never done laying!
Here's another orb glowing in her hand.

    Tomorrow (Saturday)
Wilma and Maggie, Willie and Anna and Tom
Will come with pace-egg baskets
To plunder (pleading) her hoard.

7
On Easter Day, the journey is over,
   The fourteen
   Stations of the death-faring.

A boy in white is lighting the pascal candle.
   The lilies lie in the chapel window.

The old priest, entering
Is robed in white.

The people kneel, like a new wave breaking.
(But that wave, four centuries since, was drawn back
Into the loom of ocean, a glittering thread.)

pace: Easter

Good Friday: The Women of Jerusalem

Seven women at the seven gates of the city.
   One has scales on her arms from the fish market,
   One fire-flushed from the kneaded oats and the
                                   oven,
   One an old woman, the eyes broken webs,
   One comes running, water spilling from the jar on
                           her shoulder,
   Veronica plucks a shred of wool from her mouth.
   One has issued
   From a place of silver and silk and mirrors,
   A child is there, splashed with buttercups, dew,
                            dawnlight.

They sing *Magnificat*. They sing *Ave Maria*.
Their mouths are dark soon with *Dies Irae*.

       *

A cry from the city square, 'He is fallen' . . .
          'His shoulder is bruised' . . .
Then trumpet, wheel, a scatter of hooves.

       *

   The women have left the seven gates of the city.
   They stand here and there, among crowds
   On the Road of Thorns, that goes on up the hill.
   On one side a field of green corn and a vineyard.
   On one side fishnets drying in the wind.

   The Man will come soon, carrying the dead tree.

Stations of the Cross: Veronica

Close your linen-shop, Veronica.
Who buys and sells
   The day a death-sentence is given?

This young man
I saw among the palms and shouting children!
   He must carry the dead tree.

He is not riding an ass today.
He is on his face, in swirls of hot dust.

A woman says his name
Like a mother that calls her child in from play.

He can't bear that baulk further.
A countryman slopes the burden across his shoulder.

I'm a quiet woman. But I took
A napkin I wove this morning
   To the blood, thorns, dust, sweat, on his face.

The centurion thrust me back. Six soldiers
Dragged him again to his feet.

There is weeping along the road.
The town women
Think of their sons, all the Sorrows of Man.

I would (but for the guardsmen)
Gather him up from the hot stones.

I would
Weave for such a one a coat of great beauty.

God created trees
For birdsong and fruit, not for this.

Tell me, sir – I can't read –
What is the writing on the tree?
THE KING OF THE JEWS

Now the mother folds him home.
The child has never
Come back to such a sleep at evening, out of the country
fields.

Go home now, Veronica, to your looms.
In a field outside the city
See, a sower is burying seed in a furrow.

Stations of the Cross: The Good Thief

The cold Roman eye, hand on seal.
Vale. Take the thief away.

'You carry your own tree, Jimmy . . .'
Another gallowsbird behind.
One ahead, burdened, a bruised brightness.

I've carried millstones, wine-vats, a mast.
That one was a carpenter.
His knees buckle under the heavy baulk.

My mother, poor woman, is dead.
His mother is here. Poor woman. Poor woman.

Look, Simon's come into town
With an ox to sell.
They've laid another yoke on Simon.

Veronica, seamstress. No napkin ever
Soaked up such blood and sweat.

I stagger but I don't fall.
The sneak-thief plods like a mule.
The bright one, he's down again.

Those women! Miriam, Judith, Esther
Go home, sing over your cradles.
Sing among looms and pots.

Below, cornfields and vineyards.
A third time, fallen,
He tastes golden dust.

The soldiers won't bother, I think,
Haggling over my coat.
No scarecrow would wear a rag like that.

Silence – curses – from cross and cross.
From the mid-ark
A dove wings out into the blackest storm.

Thrust of lance into heart-root.
The soldiers are coming with mallets
To break the legs of the thieves.

The eyes of the mother
Drown all the world in pity and love.
The hammer beats on my knee.

That the hands of such a woman
Fold me gravewards,
Bear me and all men in her folds of light.

Easter in an Island

1   Pace Eggs

They cross the hill with their little baskets
To farm after farm
And the farm wife sets a warm egg in every basket.

The dog barks at the troop of children
From the end of the barn.

And maybe there's one old wife
Who shuts her door against them.

And Lisa takes them in to her fire
Out of the cold wind
And butters a bannock for them, with rhubarb jam.

And the cock rears high on the barn roof.
He rings out rage or triumph.

2   Chocolate Eggs

'What'll they think of next?'
Says Tom at the village shop
To the sweetie traveller from Dundee –
        'Chocolate eggs' . . .

And the traveller in the bowler hat
Writes in his order book,
'One score chocolate Easter eggs
For Thomas Yule, merchant, Selskay.'

Then Bella Smith came in for a stone of sugar
For the spring brewing.

3 *Muirburn*

On the hill three young men with heather torches
At the muirburn.
Drifts of smoke over heather and peat-bog.
After sunset
The hill is scarred red with fires.

And the three men at the inn
Washing the muirburn soot out of their throats.

4 *Spring-cleaning*

What's wrong with the women?
Out! Get Out! they rage at their men.

They're on their knees with bucket and clout
Till the stone floor
Shines like blue mirrors.
And the chaff beds are beaten outside till stour
Darkens the sun,
And their panes glitter like stars.
(There's been a mighty rout of spiders.)

Even the cat has left this madhouse
And sits, tail lashing, on the planticru wall.

At tea-time, it's as if the first wind of time
Had blown through every house.

Schoolgirls, in troops,
Drift home, spilling first daisies.

stour: dust

5 Hot Cross Buns

No ordinary cookies, today;
Richan the baker
Has shaken a pot of spice into the dough
And every blob of dough
He crosses with strips of damp pastry.

'There!' says Richan the baker.
'Let the hearth-women try to do that –
Them and their mud-tasting bannocks' ...
And he blows up the bakehouse fire.

Jimmy the apprentice
Carries a smoking basket of hot-cross buns
Out to the grocery van.

6 Saturday

The *Beagle*, *Skarfie*, *Trust*, fishing boats
Had no longing for the West
On Good Friday.
Today's a fine day for the haddocks, too
But the twelve fishermen
Sit on the rock, smoking their pipes.

Tomorrow is Sabbath.

Come Monday morning, we'll hear
Their blue-gray shouts along the shore,
Shriek of keel upon stone,
The sails yearning westward into a sea-growl
Before the lark is up.

7   *Gravedigger*

There's no other way. Flaws, gravedigger,
Has been in the kirkyard all day
Making a grave for the tinker
Who died a quarry-death.

The end of the road, he says
With every spadeful of clay.

It comes to us all, puffing his pipe
To the sculpted marble over the laird's wife,
To the blue sea-stone for the fisherman's boy.
　　(They ended the journey last month)

The wonder of it, the wonder,
Turning a skull with his spade.
Lark song spatters a hundred gravestones.

In at the gate come seven men
And one is wound in the long silence.

A Landlady in Emmaus

I was just thinking, 'I hope Tom and Ed
Haven't got themselves in the jail' –
I knew they'd been going to the meetings
And when they could find the time
They'd been following this preacher through the
villages,
Driving here and there in their van –
When there came Tom's knock at the door
(I know Tom's knock, it's different
From the soldiers' or the taxman's knock).
I tell you, I *was* glad . . .

Now the preacher's dead, him
That put such disturbance on the countryside,
And took Tom from forge and anvil
And Ed from his sheep, days on end,
Maybe they'll settle down now,
Get married, and put a little by
For a house and a garden, and be good citizens
Like they were meant to be.
I was never tired of telling them that.
That's what I thought, when I heard the news on the
radio.

I like Tom and Ed, they've been boarders two years
At this establishment, but since the preacher
Came to the city they've been in their rooms
One night in seven, if that.
And they're not what they were, I don't know how
But they're different, more cheerful and careless
And they never come home drunk
And they'll stop to talk to a child or a bird in the dust
And once I saw them with the blind man

Whose eyes (they say) are full of light now.
Well, I thought, going to them meetings
Is better than being with the football hooligans.

Then the newspaper headlines – TERRORIST LEADER
ARRESTED,
The road-blocks, the blackout, identity cards,
Soldiers everywhere, the city in turmoil,
One day all flags and songs, the next
Black with guns, loudspeakers, lamentation,
And men scattered to the caves and the bitter shores.
Then trial and sentence, and the execution on the
hillside
– It was all on TV, with theologians and politicians
Telling us what it all meant –
It was then I worried most about my lodgers.
'They're only hangers-on at best,' I thought,
'The authorities won't worry about the likes of them' . . .
Still, you never know, in a time of troubles
The guilty go free, the innocent are caught in the net.

I set a supper that night for *three*, not two,
A bottle of wine and a new loaf,
Just what Tom and Ed always liked
After a long day of sun and dust,
One from the smithy, one from the sheepfold.
I didn't like it, a stranger
They'd given a lift to on the dark road.
You never know who's a spy or informer
Nowadays, and the man's head was hooded
And the one candle (there was a power-cut too)
Hollowed his face, and lit
Only the strong beautiful mouth.
Tom said, 'You're welcome. Break the bread.'
. The words of blessing
Came like the first and the last music.

He stretched out a wounded hand
To the loaf on the plate.
The cowl fell back. I saw then
The crusted ore and rubies at the temple.

Trinity

Sailing to Greenland

Cargo

Stowed trees into *Blue Swan*, three days
At Hamnavoe, brought thence
From Man and Tummel
    Shipwrights in Iceland
Might make keels of, powerful ocean curves,
    Stout rooftrees in plenty
For craftsman and carver.

Less trees in that island
    Leif told us – cook and lookout –
Than in Hoy, Papay, even.

Wood is weighed against thick silver.

Fiddler

Shetlanders offered us dried fish.
    'Take Lowrie, fiddler
For cheer on the bleak ocean' . . .

We knew, before Torshavn
    The boy Lowrie to be an apprentice music-man
Bundled from Yell
For wool-reft, creel-reft, night-goer
    Among the shore houses.

Oarsmen blocked ears against a screeching.
    Thorfinn had that boy
More at the bailing-can than fiddle.

Whalemeat

We had to guard our cargo seven nights
    In Faroe, such hunger was
    For oak, sycamore, larch.

Gorges rose against raw whalemeat,
Throats rasped from that ale.

Ballad-making in a long barn.
    Lowrie returned with a hundred verses,
The bird at his shoulder
    Shrieked farewells to Mykines.

Monkfish

Blue Swan had sailed Rinansay down
    Three days after Easter.

Leif shaded eyes east and west
    For wolf ships, Vikings.

Sven and Rolf released monkfish jaws
From bone hooks, a hundred.

We gave heads and tails of monkfish
    To a ship of Irish monks.
They gave us a blessing
Cleaner and brighter than a jumping salmon.

Trond, helmsman, asked for a strong curse
On the demon in Lowrie's fiddle.

Vale

In Reykjavik we had bitter news.
    Three ships from Norway
Had held east from Iceland
At Pentecost, the holds empty
    By half a Norwegian forest.

Our skipper: 'Icelandic trick
    To get the timber for next to nothing,
    For a cartload of ewe-cheese heavy as stone' . . .
We held west. Lowrie
Made a tune 'Farewell to Iceland'.

Floes

The easterly storm, two floes
    We sailed between, ice jaws
Would have cracked our ship like a nut,
Rudder broken, Bui from Rousay
    Licked by a green sea-tongue, lost.

First sun-glitters. Quiet waters.

Then Sven, 'Bergs are far south this spring.
    Better we should point prow
At Vinland, rim of the golden bowl'.

Angel bird

We heard Mass with Greenlanders
In the bishop's kirk, two days
    After good trading for bear skins, walrus tusks.
Much eagerness for the Scottish timber.

We covered the ale casks.
    This had been told us,

Greenlanders, after drink, roamed like wolves.

On Trinity Sunday, between
Boys singing *Sanctus* and *Benedictus*
    Lowrie made an interlude.
    The old bishop said,
'That boy's bird-shaped box,
Surely an angel lives in it'.

Crusaders in Orkahowe

Norwegians wintered in Orkney in 1151, before the great northern crusade under Earl Rognvald II of Orkney (1151–4). They carved runes in the burial chamber Maeshowe, called by them Orkahowe.

1
Ghosts guard here a great treasure, men say.
    The Orkahowe ghosts
Drove some men mad, they
Shelterers from a blizzard.
Guardians of the gold,
    Have the hoard keys ready for certain seamen.
We are coming today to see you.

2
Prise up a roof slab. Look,
    Morning sun
Falls like a sword through stone-dust.
Lower the ropes,
    A knot here and there, hand holds.
    We have lit three torches,
Frail flung flames outside in sun and wind.

3
What, Rolf, you can't stay?
    Rolf bleats like a goat on Orkahowe.
    I'd clean forgot. I owe
The Appiehouse farmer in this parish
    For three cheeses his wife made me
At Lammas-time last . . .
    Other business is of high importance
To a man with a gray face and shaking hands.

4
Who's to go in first? Who
Will climb down into this grave?
Ingibiorg's boyfriend, will you
Kiss the cheek of the ghosts?
(No redness on their mouths)
Hermund is putting
A biting edge on the last axe.
Well, we are pilgrims, Jerusalem-bound.
See how the ghosts will shrink
When I write JERUSALEM on the wall.

5
I'm tired of salt, fish guts, tar, gulls.
Since Trondheim
I've slept in a sack on deck.
I have no skill in writing runes
But I will hold a torch for Ragn
Who cuts pure and deep,
Far from the flung spray off Unst.

6
Thin skull, a ruckle
Of long thin bones.
How long, lady, since your eye sockets
Brimmed with light?
Milk lass and weaving lass
Stood higher than you, lady
The day your loveliness
Was laid in this stone bed.
Be glad, poor ghost.
Ragn intends to write a stone poem for you.

7
Maybe it was last winter
Thieves took gold from the finger bones.

We are too late, brothers.
But I think it was a thousand winters ago
    Men with small imagination
Deprived poor sailors of silver.
Today we are writing axe-poems
    Longer-lasting than any yellow ore.

The Laird and the Three Women

Clay curves shining from my plough
Says Tom the ploughboy

I must harrow a hill, come sun, come snow
Says Tom the servant

My fingers let the good seed flow
Says Tom the tenant

Now the first brairds green and grow
Says Tom the crofter

Gold winds round the scarecrow blow
Says Tom the horseman

I own whatever I reap and mow
Says Tom of the Glebe

My tranced harvesters come and go
Says Tom the corn-man

Ale and bread in my big barn stow
Says Tom the laird

                    *

Star and icicle pierce me through
Says Tom, bewintered

                    *

Time to light him a candle now
Say the three women

brairds: first shoots of a crop

75

A Poem for *Shelter*

Who has set his house among the stars?
Who has made his dwellingplace the
     dawn, and the western glory
     where the sun goes down?
Who has instructed the eagle to
     establish his place on a
     mountain ledge near the snow
And the little mouse in a cell safe from
     hawk and ploughshare?
The albatross dwells in the house of
     blizzard and spindrift,
     south of Cape Horn, he
     'sleeps on his own wings'.
What has The Word chosen, to be his
     house among men?
A byre, shared with winter creatures
But that was to set at naught
     princes' palaces and the
     pyramids of dead
     jewelled pharaohs.
The true inheritors of earth are
     the people
Who desire to live in simple houses
Not too close together but enough
     for neighbourliness
Where a family may sit at peace
     under its own rooftree.

There is enough stone in Alps, Urals,
     Himalayas
To quarry a million cornerstones.
But always, in winter, under
     stars like thorns
The wanderers wait, the breakers of icicles,
     the homeless ones.

Saturday: A Boy in Hamnavoe

Penny

The Saturday penny
    Sang a small boy in Hamnavoe
What sweetness can I buy
To glue my teeth
    Between two sea breaths?
    I could buy
A sherbet dab from Janetta Sinclair
Or a Guilio Fuggacia ice-cream slider.

Sweeties

He went among shop windows,
    A small sweetaholic.
The new Mars Bars taste like heaven
But they cost twopence
Twopence for Rachel Smith's claggam too.

Chocolate and Lemonade

A bottle of lemonade
    Is only for picnics at The Tender Tables
With ginger snaps, abernethy biscuits.
I'd do a lot for a bar of Cadbury's
    Or Fry's chocolate cream.
Why do such bits of heaven
    Have to cost *two*pence?

Cinema

A penny doesn't go far
    When it costs fourpence
To sit in the cave of shifting shadows

With Tom Mix or Charlie Chaplin.
The 'Wizard' on Tuesday –
*Two*pence again – that everlasting barrier.

Olive Oil

An old gentle-tongued lady
      At a close end:
'Georgie, will you get a bottle of olive oil
From the chemist?
My man needs olive oil for his stomach.
And here's a shilling for going.'

Silver Star

A shilling! I held a star
      On my finger-ends.
Not a bird flew faster
      From chemist's to close-end with olive oil
Than the boy dying of sweet-lack.
      She was no old woman, she
Was an angel, and her man
– So rusty inside! – had the gentlest of smiles.

Debauch

All that Saturday a debauch
      Of bon-bons, butternuts, Gowans's
American Cream Soda,
Ice-cream to make the teeth shiver,
      A liquorice stick, slab of Highland Cream.
Why aren't you eating your good mince and tatties? ...
      Languor at evening
Under the shifting cinema shafts,
Wallace Beery, a hoodlum, on Death Row.

claggam: home-made toffee

Attie Campbell
1900–1967

Where do you wander now, old friend?
Where do you drink?
Few inns better than Hamnavoe bar,
Few better stories, I think.
Is there a star
Stirred with laughter that has no end

A million light-years beyond the Milky Way
Where Villon and Burns,
Falstaff and slant-eyed Li Po
Order their nectar by turns
(No 'Time, gents' there, no drinker has to pay)
And words immortal gather head and flow?

For that far glim you'd crank your aged car,
But that the faint bell-cry
Of tide changing in Hoy Sound,
The corn surges that salve the deep plough-wound,
Would draw you home to where you are
At Warbeth, among the dead who do not die.

Agricultural Show: Dounby

We are the old men. Days scatter,
Husks on a threshing floor.
 Shall we look on the black
 Or on the bright solstice again,

Or go in at darkling Barleycorn doors
Or surprise April through the green gate?
 Time gathers to a fullness; then
 He's wise who turns gravely,

Raises a hand in thanks for the story
And leaves in peace under the first star.
 We linger it out. Better men
 Have gone when the sun stood over the hill.

We would linger it out, earthbound
Till ice-blades shred us to scarecrows.
 We would plead with winter,
 Barn bound, for one more furrow-time.

Too late, too late. The last stook
Is long in the yard. Light tarnishes.
 To wish back the sun
 Sets ice on a child's lips,

Some farmer's son – He's there, look,
Outside the gate of a 'fair field
 Full of folk', the festive
 Dance of the nine parishes.

Turn at the gate. Bless his urgency,
This new word in the story of Orc.
 Bless the supplanter.
 Lay sunset lingerings on

That hill of blond surges, they hallow
Tomorrow's harvester. And see,
   The horse we banished from our hills
   Drifts delicately to his handful of grass.

Pomona Inn, Finstown, Orkney
(founded by John Finn, Peninsular veteran)

I'm tired of Spain and musket and cannonball,
Said Finn the soldier

I'll be like Napoleon and go to a lonely isle,
Said Irish Finn

I journeyed to 'the islands of the whale',
Said Finn the soldier

What work for a veteran soldier on Heddle Hill?
Said Irish Finn

Ploughmen, I think, like a jar or two of ale,
Said Finn the soldier

And here there's no shebeen to sip or swill,
Said Irish Finn

No place to go when their wives scold and shrill,
Said Finn the soldier

I'll have a word with the man that keeps the mill,
Said Irish Finn

To sell me some sacks of malt, his overspill,
Said Finn the soldier

To where I'll build an ale-house, wall by wall
Said Irish Finn

And there in peace travellers may drink their fill
Said Finn the soldier

Twixt fire and lamp and barrel and rattling till,
Said Irish Finn

Lovers may linger long when love goes ill,
Said Finn the soldier

And mourners warm them from the kirkyard chill,
Said Irish Finn

I'll be your good host, come you when you will,
Said Finn the soldier

I've beaten the cannon to pewter mugs – all's well,
Sang Finn the landlord.

Robert Rendall
Orkney Poet

You have been here, before your latest birth,
    (Cheeks, at the pan-pipes, apple-red and round!)
Followed your wooden plough through Attic earth,
    And pulled your lobsters from a wine-dark sound.

Now for a flicker of time you walk once more
    In other islands, under geese-gray skies,
And note, on Birsay hill and Birsay shore,
    The year's glad cycle out of ancient eyes.

O happy grove of poetry! where the soul
    Is never sundered from the laughing blood,
But sweetly bound, harmonious and whole
    In covenant with animal and god.

But I came here unheralded, and meet
Masquers and shadows mingling in the street.

One Star in the West

To have got so far, alone
Almost to the seventieth stone
    Is a wonder.
    There was thunder

A few miles back, a storm-shaken
Hill and sea, the bridge broken
    (The bright fluent
    Burn a bruised torrent.)

But all cleared, larks were singing
Again, the April rain ringing
    Across the sown hills,
    Among the daffodils.

The road winds uphill, but
A wonder will be to sit
    On the stone at last –
    One star in the west.

A Work for Poets

To have carved on the days of our vanity
A sun
A ship
A star
A cornstalk

Also a few marks
From an ancient forgotten time
A child may read

That not far from the stone
A well
Might open for wayfarers

Here is a work for poets –
Carve the runes
Then be content with silence